Dimwit iPhone 12 Pro Max Mastering

iPhone 12 Pro User Guide for Beginners with Comprehensive Manual to Get Started with Apple Siri Smartphone

Jim Wood

This book or any portion thereof may not be reproduced or used in any manner whatsoever without the express written permission of the publisher except for the use of brief quotations in a book review.

You are welcome to join the Fan's Corner, here

Dimwit iPhone 12 Pro Max Mastering

iPhone 12 Pro User Guide for Beginners with Comprehensive Manual to Get Started with Apple Siri Smartphone

Jim Wood

Disclaimer

The advice and strategies found within may not be suitable for every situation. This work is sold with the understanding that neither the author nor the publisher is held responsible for the results accrued from the advice in this book.

Contents

Part 1

INTRODUCTION AND BASICS

Introduction

This guide was formatted in such a way to help you use all the powerful features that come with your iPhone as quickly as possible so that you do not have to spend long hours with a manual when trying to use your new phone casually and simply in a format that is different from what is obtained from many of our competitors.

Getting an iPhone can be a thrilling and yet intimidating experience. On the one hand, it's like getting a new gadget, especially when it is one of the best phones' money can buy with its amazing packed full features.

This most sought-after iPhone 12 Pro Max guide has helped thousands of users learn how to use the iPhone 12 Pro Max which is believed to be one of the fastest and powerful phones on the market at the time this book was written.

This bestselling guide provides you with the right tips, tricks, shortcuts, and workaround that are all aimed at turning you into an iPhone 12 Pro Max master. The guide was written to help you take better advantage of its trouble-free setup, velvety haptics, and smooth buttery performance.

This is the easy-to-follow step by step guide you have been looking for.

Dimwit iPhone 12 Pro Max Mastering is a user guide for iPhone 12 Pro Max for beginners, designed specifically to ease up the process of comprehensive learning on how to use the iPhone 12 Pro Max even by beginners, as well as for those who are already users of iPhone.

This book covers all the necessary topics needed to know the different features of the new iPhone 12 Pro Max. From learning how to start up the phone, to the in-depth features. This book covers all the essential knowledge needed to be known by the users.

The main purpose of this book is to make it easy to use the phone for iPhone 12 Pro Max users and other iPhone users as well. This book contains step by step and detailed information about the functions and features present in the iPhone 12 Pro Max, making it easier for a non-iPhone user as well to get started using the iPhone 12 Pro Max right away, without thinking too much about understanding the usage of the iPhone.

This book mainly focuses on the features of the new iPhone 12 Pro Max; however, it may be used as a guide for other iPhone models as well to understand the basic settings and features of the other iPhones. The iPhone models that this book can also be used as a guide for include: iPhone 12 Pro Max, iPhone 12 Pro, iPhone 12, Mini iPhone 12, iPhone 11 Pro Max, iPhone 11 Pro, iPhone 11, Mini iPhone 11, iPhone XR, iPhone XS, iPhone XS Max, iPhone X, also for iPhone SE(2nd generation), iPhone 8, iPhone 8 Plus, iPhone 7, iPhone 7 Plus, iPhone 6s, iPhone 6s Plus, and iPhone SE (1st generation).

Well, some of the iPhone models aren't eligible to be upgraded to iOS 14.1 in some of the regions of the world. It's better to check the compatibility of the upgrading version of your iPhone or the current iOS version of your iPhone.

To see your model, go to Settings > General > About Phone; where you see Get information about your phone. It will provide complete information on the model name, capacity, and storage.

Other information you will find will include name, iOS software version, part and model numbers (to the right of the model, the part number is present, and to see the number of the model; tap the part number), cellular network, serial number, number of songs, vids, apps, and photos, Wi-Fi and Bluetooth addresses,

IMEI (International Mobile Equipment Identity), ICCID (Indicated Circuit Card Identifier, or Smart Card) for GSM networks, MEID (mobile equipment identifier) for CDMA networks, Modem firmware, Carrier settings, and Legal (which includes legal license, notices, warranty, and RF exposure info).

This book provides you with the opportunity to demand 100% of your iPhone capability by covering all the necessary information and providing you with an easy to use guide about the Camera of the iPhone 12 Pro Max features and various similar other savoring features of the new iPhone 12 Pro Max.

The necessity for an iPhone user to have this book is 10/10. To have a better experience of using your new iPhone 12 Pro Max, dive into this book, and get the most of your new iPhone 12 Pro Max.

The main purpose of creating this book is to help the users; whether they are the old users or the newbies, to learn, and to take the full benefit of their iPhone 12 Pro Max. Besides, the book helps the users to get easy access to its in-depth features and functions provided that they won't be rendered astray while using the phone.

Moreover, if the user gets stuck on a particular feature this book will help to take him out of it, making the knowledge as feasible for its readers as possible within a limited amount of time.

This book is merely an hour's read. With the help of the table of contents drawn at the beginning, it becomes easy for the users to jump to specific topics they are looking to be guided on. In a very comprehensive way, everything is written and explained for the users to enjoy most of the amazing and brand-new features of iOS 14.1, the software version installed in the new iPhone 12 Pro Max.

The contents of this group are thoroughly analyzed and enter the book to meet the best possible need of learning all about iPhone 12 Pro Max and simultaneously other iPhone models as well.

Those who have grabbed a hold of this book may find it a piece of cake to learn the new and amazing features and get all the benefits of their iPhones. After reaching the end of this book the reader will be able to access all the mandatory, as well as small functions, present on the phone.

With the extensive knowledge and elaboration of every topic, the reader will find answers to every question that was previously nagging in his/her mind. This is what the book promises. For its readers, it is going to be easier than internet searches and thus; readers will no longer have to tirelessly run through the internet to find the particular tool or to access the information about a specific feature of their iPhones. It is designed to save time and effort.

About iPhone

Apple Inc. was founded in 1976 by the amazing Steve Job, Steve Wozniak, and Ronald Wayne; its first public appearance was made in the year 1976. Apple has traveled a far distance from the very first launch of the iMac in 1998 to now producing and selling millions of products. The first generation of the iPhone was launched in the year 2007, and thus iPhone has become the fastest-growing product of Apple by launching its newest models every year and upgrading iOS versions over the years. The models of iPhone that have been launched so far are iPhone (1st generation), 3G, 3GS, iPhone 4, 4S, iPhone 5, 5S, 5C, iPhone 6, 6 Plus, 6S, 6S Plus, SE (1st), iPhone 7, 7Plus, 7S, iPhone 8, 8 Plus, iPhone X, XS, XS Max, XR, iPhone 11, 11 Pro, 11 Pro Max, SE (2nd), iPhone 12, 12 Pro, and 12 Pro Max. Their features have been enhanced and a vast variety of new features have been introduced since the launch of the first iPhone. The iOS versions have been improved over the years, making many cool functions available while easing up the use of the phone. The growing market for iPhone promises really good fortune for the makers and developers of the iPhone.

In a recent sales report of November 1, 2018, more than 2.2 billion iPhones were stated to be sold up-till then, and now the ratio must be higher of course; iPhone is made user friendly, it's easy to understand. With the latest models, you can do things that you would have never imagined before. The look of the iPhone has also been improved over the years, making it cooler than ever before.

iPhone 12 Pro Max (What makes it unique?)

The iPhone 12 Pro Max was launched on the 13th of November 2020. With its mind-blowing features, it is taking on the market with pace. The company called it a leap year, meaning the new iPhone 12 Pro Max has got it all piled up in one single smartphone.

Being the smartest of its type it offers 5G cellular data service with the boldest chipset ever, the Apple A14 Bionic with increased 40% more transistors rev up speed to improve the battery life as well, installed with new ISP Dolby vision recording, with 6.7 inches super Retina XDR display with 2778-by-1285 pixel resolution, surrounded by the ever strongest ceramic sheet, which is made by molding Nano-ceramic crystals into the glass, making it the toughest, so that even if it is dropped multiple times, you don't have to worry about its strong body that is made more credible now.

Besides this, the dual ion-exchange formula is used to shield the screen from getting scratched even with very rough and tough everyday use. The side body is made of stainless steel of surgical grade to keep the look intact even after many years of use. The best IP68 water-resistance is used in the device, preventing even a drop to enter the system. It is made available in four amazing colors, which are pacific blue, graphite, gold, and silver color.

The LiDAR scanner AR is present in the iPhone 12 Pro Max to measure the speed of reflection of light after hitting the objects; the purpose is to construct a map of your current space within nanoseconds.

The Pro camera system is installed with features that help in enhancing the low-light mode, capable of capturing pictures in the dim-light with high professionalism with the help of the incredible night-mode.

The new iOS can make 5000 adjustments per second; LiDAR gives up to 6x faster autofocus in dim light. The front selfie camera is 12MP with f/2.2, 23mm wide (1/3.6 inches). There are three main-cameras of 12MP, 12MP, and 12 MP with f/1.6, 26mm, f/2.4, and f/2.6 apertures relatively. The phone is available in 3 different storage variants, 128 GB, 256 GB, and 512 GB all with 6GB RAM. The Dolby recording vision now has 60 times more colors; capturing 700 million colors for a real lifelike video experience, which is a general format used by film studios.

The new turbo chargeable has fastened the wireless charging. The iOS14 is the latest version to enhance the features and has built new creative shortcuts to make it as easy as possible in reaching various apps. The app clips have been introduced to help with the usage of any part of an app quickly

The newly designed widgets will help in popping up the info you want on your home screen. Pinned conversations available in the messages put the people most chatted with at the top right. The privacy policy is strict and not even a single piece of information about the user is revealed, the FaceID data is kept on the iPhone, iOS reveals the privacy terms of the Apps before being downloaded. While using Apple pay, it doesn't show the user's card number or any kind of information to any third external party or the merchants.

The best part about the iPhone 12 Pro Max is the initiative of the iPhone in reducing the emission of carbon particles; the iPhone has made sure that it works best for the environment. It is providing extensive worldwide coverage by supporting 20 5G bands and up to 30 LTE bands.

iOS 14 (What's new?)

iOS 14 has brought a new look to the daily used features, easing them up and making them look more attractive than before. The apps have become private, feasible, and easier. Starting with the widgets on the home screen, it has been redesigned to reach out to what you need at a glance.

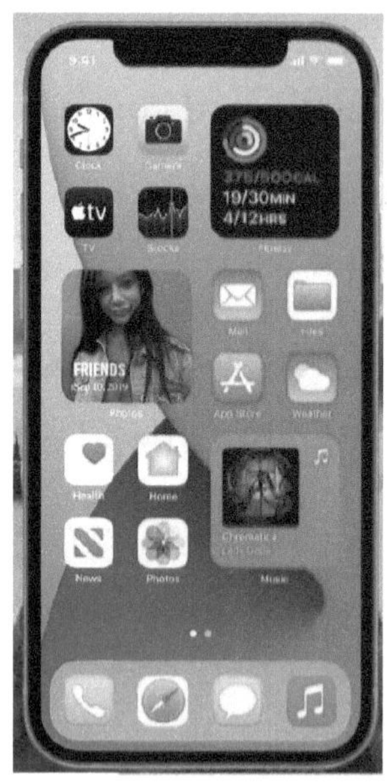

It is now easy to add any feature you'd like to add to your home screen and arrange them. The best part about adding widgets is "stacking"; you can stack the apps you like to use the most and the exact widget will pop up at the right time daily.

A new API option is made available to developers to be able to develop innovative widgets and take advantage of the redesigned widgets. A mesmerizing feature of Siri's suggestion widget uses an on-device intelligence and with its help shows actions related to the things you have been using and might like to use.

The widget gallery has a central space for all the widgets from Apple and third parties and they pop up on the most used base. The availability of the widget in every size makes it easier to find. The fresh App library organizes the Apps into one or more sections based on their types.

To save time looking for a particular App with the most used App, Apple has made it to just be a tap away, by easing up the search for you by tapping on the search bar above, so that you are able to easily find the app of your choice as the menu drops down in alphabetical order while the new apps downloaded from the app store shifts directly to the App library.

iOS 14 has solved the main problem of call interference by compacting the calls, so they don't take up the whole space on the screen. Now they are shown at the top even if the call is on any third-party app like Skype etc. With the help of a developer API. The picture in picture effect is pretty cool which means you can continue watching your videos while using another App.

You can also resize the picture in the picture window and it can be moved to any corner, can be zoomed-in, and zoomed-out. Siri is now compacted as well, with a beautiful small layout; it gives the required information without disturbing the task you were indulged in. Searching through the Apps is made at the fingertips.

Pinning up the nine most important conversations in the messages is another cool feature offered by iOS 14. Tagging someone has been made easier in a group chat, and it can also be customized to give notification only when your name is mentioned, or you can reply to a particular message in a group conversation. And a profile picture can also be chosen for the group.

You can apply and make your own avatar using 20 different images, according to your profession or passion, which is a funky tool that allows many different faces, accessories, and head-wears to reflect a perfect personality. With iOS 14 the locations have become easier to approach than ever before, and their discovery has come hand in hand.

The guides available for the perfect eating spots and traveling guides are made with the help of trusted brands and partners. The auto-updating is turned on in the guides section to make sure you get the latest recommendations as soon as a new and reliable place is opened in the area. Translation App of the iOS 14 affords trouble-free chatting after being enabled; it can translate text in 11 different languages privately; the most convenient part is that can be enabled offline as well. Here is a tip for saving translations in the favorites for simple access later.

The attention mode enlarges the translated text, making it trouble-free to read and write. As popularly known; Siri is used for getting on-hand information about everything and helping out with performing actions. The new compact design has taken its functions to an extra level by getting things done quickly without losing the context of your work. It has 20x more facts and information than it had three years ago, the knowledge range is wider than it was ever before, as it can now use a web browser as well to answer the questions no matter how complicated. There is a new feature of sending audio messages via Siri for a better experience.

The home App is available with intelligent management service, provided with more security. There is much automation suggested in a list for better use also. A new prioritization in the home status is introduced to sort out the list of things that you need the most so that you can easily control them. Many adaptive lights change according to the temperature throughout the day when enabled. The defined activity zones help to focus on the area with the mobile's camera and when some activity is performed in that area; the user gets notified. Video cameras and doorbells can detect the people previously tagged in the photos App.

It is totally up to the user to simply tag the person and get notified. Safari is another upgraded and faster feature with iOS 14 to make web browsing more reliable, hasty and effortless, with its wide range of research and the response is also improved. It can also translate different websites in seven different languages provided with a shortcut button to translate the page supported by Safari's translation skills. It also gives warning about insecure passwords and can detect if the web page you are browsing has some privacy issue, preventing the trackers from following your device.

Now, cars can be unlocked and get started with your iPhone, in short CarPlay has completely changed the relationship between your car and the phone. Keys can even be shared with family or friends it can be done for a limited period as well as for a longer period, well, CarPlay is also now affording new App types. AirPods are offering a phenomenal listening experience with iOS 14 as it has a few new tricks, surrounding all the nearby sounds now; the battery notification easily tells about AirPods battery running out on the top of the screen. Also, the automatic switching between the iPhone and iPad is made available for a wonderful and timeless experience. AirPods audio can be adjusted to account for hearing differences, headphones accommodation offers to amplify soft sounds and thus making the other sounds clearer and crispier just like in the headphones.

Audio sharing for Apple TV allows you to connect two sets of AirPods to a 4k Apple TV to watch movies together without breaking the tranquility of others. With App clips, there is a chance of taking more advantage of the Apps in the App store as it is available to discover at just the time you need it and about a specific task in the App you are looking for. Log in to the Apps that use Apple's ID and then buy things from the Apps that use Apple Pay for payment with just one tap.

The most important part of iOS 14 is its provision of privacy for all the data and information, it secures the users' data and doesn't share it with any third party; giving the user full control over whoever they would like to share it with. The full understanding of the privacy practices of the Apps is always displayed to the users when they want to download from the App store. If an app is using the phone's camera or microphone or indicator, known as a result recording indicator, appears at the top of the screen and you can even check later in the control center if the App has used your camera or microphone recently.

While logging into participating Apps the sign in with Apple is made available for one less password use. Sharing your approximate location and not the current or exact location is also the safest method for the smaller Apps. Apple Arcade has got many new games and you can easily play your games through your Mac, iPhone, iPad, and Apple TV by turning on the continue playing feature. Apple Cash Family can now be used for people under the age of 18, the family members, friends, or anyone can send them allowances and they can use it wherever the Apple Pay is accepted, a perfect experience to do with parental controls.

The Augmented reality, AR kit 4 has made it easy for the developers to set up AR experiences making it delightful for them in every way. The fastest ever shots in the camera has been introduced with a new exposure and compensation control for a wonderful focused shot. The exposure value can be locked while separately locking the camera exposure. The newly made game center makes it easier and quicker than before to play and find thousands of games with friends and family.

A brand-new feature that helps in maintaining the sleeping goals has been introduced in the health App. The hearing feature enables you to keep the track of the volume levels and their impact on your hearing. Photos and videos can be well organized with the new navigation feature and can be found easily. The notes have been improved by the provided help to help in finding and scanning the notes so that users can stay focused on the content.

iOS 14 has made it possible to set any third-party App as the default email or browser App. In voice memos, it becomes possible to enhance the quality of recording audios, and also the ability to have the recordings organized. Being informed about the extreme weather conditions and staying informed about upcoming weather reports is the best feature to be introduced.

Chapter 1

A Basic Guide

Setting up the phone

The new iPhone 12 Pro Max can be set up using an internet connection. It can also be set up using the computer. To prepare to set up your iPhone, you must have these things:

1. Wi-Fi available or cellular data service.

2. Your Apple ID and password or you can use the one you had in your previous iPhone.

3. Additionally, if you want to make an Apple Pay account, you can add your debit card information or your credit card during the setup.

4. Previous iPhone or backup device if you're going to transfer the data, and the android device if you want to transfer data from it.

a. *Powering on and the earliest set up:*

1. First of all, press and keep pressed the side button which is the sleep and wake button until the Apple logo appears. However, in case your phone doesn't turn on then you might have to charge your battery or at the end of the book; extra support is provided in case of the iPhone not turning on.

2. You can either simply tap Set up manually and keenly follow the instructions that come next.

3. Or if you have an iPhone model that runs on iOS 13 it is compatible with iOS 14, and you can automatically set up your new device using **QuickStart** by simply putting your old device closer to your new one. With this, a card appears on the screen asking to transfer all the data from the old

device to the new one and continue using the old Apple ID (if in case it doesn't then make sure your device's Bluetooth is turned on). You'll then have to point your old device's camera to the new device's camera (if your new device's camera doesn't turn on then tap "Authenticate Manually" and follow the upcoming instructions). Using your old Apple ID you'll be asked to enter your 6 digit passcode (if you have more than one device then you might be asked to enter multiple passcodes of other devices as well), then your phone will be set up in no time. But for this time-saving trick, you will be needed to at least have an iOS 11 or later version. If your phone isn't already updated, then upgrade it to the latest version to enjoy this effortless setup. After that, you'll go through the rest of the process of setting up the Face ID, etc. Within no time, your new device will set up. This way most of the settings are transferred; including the arrangement of your home screen. But it may take some time to re-download all your previous Apps. These Apps are shown arranged in the form of bundles, but re-downloading takes place every time you download an app from the app store; the phone acquires a unique version of the app suitable for the model. A Tip: You should create a backup in the old device or upgrade your backup first before transferring the data.

4. There is another method of transferring data using a wired connection it is called "device-to-device migration". You can choose if the wireless connection is slow or somehow congested. It includes the following steps:

i.   First of all, put the lightning USB 3 camera adapter to power via its lightning port. The adapter must be 12W or higher power.

ii.   After that, connect the lightning power to the USB 3 camera adapter to the existing iPhone.

iii.   Then plug the lightning to the USB cable into your iPhone 12 Pro, Max connects its other end to the adapter as well.

iv.   Then continue following the above-mentioned steps of transferring the data.

5. For blind people or people having low vision, there is an option; they have to press the side button thrice on the iPhone 12 Pro Max. Also, zoom can be activated by tapping the screen twice with three fingers.

6. To transfer things from android you need to follow the simple steps written below. These have to be done while setting up the new iPhone because if you have finished setting up the iPhone you'll then either have to manually transfer/move your data (for which the guidance is given in the 7th point) or you'll have to erase your iPhone again.

i.   To move data from an Android device to iOS, you'll first have to make sure that the following things are available.

- Make sure your android device has an internet connection.

- Plug both your android device and iPhone to power.

- Be assured that the data you're going to move to iOS would fit in it.

- To transfer bookmarks from chrome update it to its latest version.

ii. The most important thing is to download the "Move to iOS App" from Google play on your Android device that has a 4.0 or later android version.

iii. On your iPhone, follow the setup instruction, then go to the apps and screen, tap 'Move Data from Android'

iv. On your android device after turning on the Wi-Fi Move to the iOS App follow this step.

- Tap continue, after reading the terms and conditions that appears, tap 'Agree to continue further'. Just after it, tap 'next' in the top-right corner of the 'Find Your Code screen'

v.   On your iPhone, tap "Continue on the screen" called transfer/move from the Android device.

vi.   After that, wait for a few seconds for the 10 digits or 6-digit code, if during the process a message of slow internet connection on the Android device appears; ignore it.

vii.   After putting the code on the Android device, you'll have to wait for the transfer data screen to pop up.

viii.   Select all the content that you want to transfer (which may include contacts, camera photos, and videos, message history, web bookmarks, calendars, mails, and some of the free Apps that are available on both Google Play and Apple store) on your android device and tap "Next" after the android shows the process is completed wait for a few seconds until the loading bar showing up on the iOS device finishes. The process timings depend on the number of contents you're transferring.

ix.   After the loading bar on your iOS device ends, tap "Done" on your Android device, then continue setting up the iPhone using the onscreen assistance. (Note: Music, books, and pdf can only be transferred manually).

x. In case the transfer is not able to complete either due to either another App being opened or a call in progress on your Android device, the transfer of files will halt and you'll have to begin the process again, so the Move to iOS App should be kept on the screen during the whole process. If the transfer isn't taking place still, then try restarting both devices, if it still doesn't start, turn off the cellular data connection on the Android device then try again.

7. To move your content from the Android device manually to the new iPhone, follow these steps:

i. The best part about iPhone software is that it works with email providers like Google, Yahoo, Outlook or Microsoft exchange, etc. To begin, firstly add each of your email accounts to your iPhone by using the following steps:

- The step of adding an email account to your new iPhone can be done both automatically and manually, to add it automatically:
  - Go to settings > Open Mail.
  - Open Add account, select your email provider.
  - Enter your email address and password.
  - After tapping Next, wait for the verifying email.
  - Select information from your email account, e.g. contacts.
  - Tap Save.
- To add an email account manually, follow these steps:
  - Go to setting > Open Mail and then accounts.
  - Open Add account, tap other (if your email provider isn't listed), then tap add an email account.

- Enter your name, email address, password, and a description of your account.
- If it's set up correctly, then simply tap done.

ii. After adding, go to settings > Passwords and Accounts, there you'll find your email.

iii. To move photos and videos manually you'll have to use a computer and then follow these steps:

- Attach your Android device to your computer, and then find your photos and videos. Usually, they're present in DCIM > camera. On the Mac, install Android file transfer and then open DCIM > camera.

- Make a folder on your computer for every photo and video that you wish to transfer.

- While disconnecting the Android device, connect your iPhone.

- On your computer simply sync your photos to your iPhone by following these steps:

- Download iCloud for windows and make sure you're logged into iCloud with the same Apple ID on every device
- Connect your device to Wi-Fi.
- Open iCloud for windows.
- Just beside photos, click options.
- Choose iCloud photos.
- Select done, then click Apply.
- Turn on iCloud Photos on all of your devices.

- After it, you can find the photos and videos on your iOS device in the Photos > albums. If the photos are still in your PC or iMac and after iCloud updates the photo library.

- On your iMac, make sure that you're signed in to your iCloud with your Apple ID and your iMac is updated to the latest macOS, set up your iCloud. Then go to System preferences > iCloud > options next to photos, then choose iCloud photos. (Note: if chosen not to turn on iCloud Photos, syncing your videos and photos manually in the finder Mac is possible.

b. Cellular service settings:

To set up the cellular data in your iPhone, you must have a physical "Nano-SIM" provided by your carrier. But first, learn how to setup 5G with your new iPhone 12 Pro Max.

A. How to use 5G with your iPhone 12 Pro Max

Firstly, for the iPhone 12 Pro Max that supports 5G, you must have:

- Cellular SIM that supports 5G.
- Asked your carrier for a 5G cellular plan.

Then you can either use your SIM from your previous iPhone or you can use the SIM provided with your iPhone if given. But you might have to ask your carrier to make your cellular plan to let your previous SIM work with a 5G network.

Secondly, you must understand what the 5G icons in the status bar represent:

- **5G:** it indicates that your 5G network is made available and can be connected to the internet. (Note: it isn't available in every area)
- **5G+:** it indicates that a higher frequency version of 5G is made available by your carrier in the region and your phone is connected over the internet. (Note: it isn't available in every area)

Thirdly the various options are available on 5G that can be optimized according to your usage to save battery life and data usage. To get these options, go to Settings > Cellular > Cellular Data Options. For dual SIM users, go to Settings > Cellular and choose SIM to change its settings. These options are:

- Voice and Data: according to the effect on the battery life choose among the following options.
  - 5G On: with this, the mobile phone uses 5G whenever it is available, resulting in the reduction of battery.

- 5G Auto: with this option the mobile phone uses 5G only when the battery is full or halfway. It disables the 5G when the phone's battery drops low.

  - LTE: for using only the LTE network, even when 5G is accessible.

- Data Mode: the following options have been made available in the data model.

  - Allow more data on 5G: as the name suggests, it will let you use the higher frequency of data for system tasks and Apps, which includes, high-quality FaceTime chat, high-resolution Apple TV videos. This particular setting allows Apple Music, songs and videos, and iOS to upgrade, and it also enables third-party Apps to use more 5G for a better experience. It is a default setting and depending upon the carrier, it has unlimited-data plans. In short, it uses a greater amount of cellular data.

- Standard: Again, as the name suggests this is a general default mode that allows a limited amount of data for FaceTime and videos but provides automatic updates in the background as well.

  - Low Data Mode: it stops any background updates and tasks to help in the reduction of cellular data and Wi-Fi.

- Data Roaming: the 5G is unavailable in every region of the world, however, many carriers around the world are still working to make the roaming support of 5G. But when you turn on the data roaming, there's a chance for you to get LTE network data or 4G while traveling and obtaining an eSIM or a local SIM card in the areas where 5G is available is possible through this.

- Here is what you can do if you're unable to see 5G in the status bar.

  - Firstly, you have to be assured that you're in an area that 5G covers. You can know about it by contacting your carrier.

- Secondly, Go to settings > Cellular > Cellular Data options. If this screen is popping up, then your 5G is enabled. But if it's not seen, then you should contact your carrier to confirm if there is support for your 5G plan.
- There is another way, put your mobile phone on airplane mode, and then turn it off.

B. Begin setting up cellular service:

iPhone 12 Pro Max supports Dual-SIM, one can be a physical Nano-SIM another one can be an eSIM, which unfortunately is not available in all the regions. (Tips: you can keep one SIM for business and the other for personal calls, make a local data plan while traveling, and keep separate the data and voice plans)

C. Installation of the Nano-SIM:

To install the Nano-SIM:

- Slide a SIM eject tool or a paper clip into the tiny hole of the SIM tray, and then press it a little until the tray ejects.
- Take it out of the iPhone.

- Put the Nano-SIM on the tray, orienting with the angled edge.

- Slide the tray back into the phone.

- If there was a Pin setup previously for the SIM, enter it as soon as it pops up on the screen. (Warning: while entering the pin, be very cautious as a little mistake can lead to the blocking of your SIM and it won't be unblocked. You'll eventually have to ask your carrier for a new SIM if the pin you entered turns out to be incorrect).

D. Setting up the cellular plan with eSIM:

A digital storage for the eSIM is made available in iPhone X and all the later versions including the new iPhone 12 Pro Max.

- First of all, to begin the setup; Go to settings > Cellular, then open Add Cellular Plan.

- You can do any of the following processes:
  - Build a new plan using a QR code given by the carrier, for which you'll have to align iPhone, so that the QR code becomes visible on the screen, or you can type the details manually. A confirmation code would be sent to you and you'll have to write it in.

- Lodge the already assigned cellular plan: you may get a notification from your carrier about an already set cellular plan, and then you'll just have to tap the "Carrier Cellular Plan" ready to be installed.

- Shift a SIM from the old iPhone to your new iPhone: Select your phone number from the list. (Tip: you'll see your number only when you're logged in to both devices with the same Apple ID).

- Open Add Cellular Plan.

- If the new plan appears as your second line, keenly follow the on-screen commands to help use both plans simultaneously.

E. Management of Cellular plans for Dual SIM:

While setting up the models with Dual SIM, the process of iPhone choosing each line can be selected. To change these settings later, you can opt for the following:

- Go to settings > Cellular

- Follow these steps:

- Open up Cellular data, and then select a default line. For the allowance of iPhone to choose itself a particular line depending on its availability and coverage, switch on "Allow Cellular Data Switching". (Note: you may be charged for roaming charges. If Data Roaming is on and out of the region of the carrier's network or if you're somewhere out of the country.)

- After it, open up the Default Voice Line, select a line.

- Just underneath Cellular Plans, tap a line, and then change a few settings such as Wi-Fi calling, calling on other devices, cellular plan label you can also change SIM Pin. You'll see the label in Phone, Messages, and Contact.

While using Dual SIM, keep these in mind:

- Don't forget to turn on Wi-Fi calling for a line that is to receive a call, while the other line is still on call. If Wi-Fi calling is turned off, then iPhone can use the Cellular Data service of the line that's on call to attend on the incoming call, and this may cost some charges. Also, the line that is being used for the call must have permitted the use of Cellular Data in your Cellular Data settings for the other line's call.

- If the Wi-Fi calling is turned off the upcoming calls may be directed to the voice mail while the other line is in use, and later you won't receive any missed call notification as well. (Note: there is a way to avoid the call from going to the voice mail by setting up conditional call forwarding (if provided by your carrier) even when a line is on another call or not in service; you can talk to your carrier for the setup).

- If the call is made from your iMac or any other device by transmitting it through your iPhone with Dual SIM, the call is through your default voice line.

- The conversations started through SMS/MMS on one line, then it can't be just switched to the other line, you'll have to delete the whole conversation and then on the other line start again. Also, some charges may apply for sending attachments and messages through the line that is not selected for cellular data.

- Hotspots both instant and Personal always use the line chosen for cellular data.

c. Access internet connection:

iPhone 12 Pro Max can be connected to the Wi-Fi or cellular network.

A. Connection to Wi-Fi network:

- Go to settings > Wi-Fi, and then switch it on.
- You'll have two options:
    - Network: enter the password, if necessary.
    - Other: you can join a hidden network by entering the name of the network, security type, and password. (Note: if the Wi-Fi sign is visible at the top, then it means that your Wi-Fi is now connected).

B. Connect to a personal Hotspot:

Hotspot of another iPhone, iMac can be connected to your iPhone if it's being shared. Its cellular internet connection can be used by you.

Simply Go to settings > Wi-Fi, and then select the device's name sharing the Hotspot.

Enter the password and find it by going to the settings > Cellular > Personal Hotspot on the device from which the Hotspot is shared.

C. Cellular Network Connection:

When the Wi-Fi is turned off or disconnected, the iPhone automatically connects to the local cellular network provided by your carrier, if it doesn't follow these steps:

- Confirm that your SIM is activated and unlocked.
- Go to Setting > Cellular
- Confirm that cellular data is turned on while using dual SIM, select cellular data, and confirm the selected line. (only one line can be selected for the cellular data)

d. Setting up Apple ID and iCloud:

Apple ID is the most important thing as it's an account that allows access to the services provided by Apple, such as the App Store, FaceTime, iCloud, iMessage, the iTunes Store, and Apple Books, etc.

iCloud provides storage for your photos, videos, documents, music, apps, etc., and updates for them across all your devices. Using iCloud, you can easily share photos, videos, and location, etc., with your friends and family. It can be used when the iPhone goes missing.

It also provides a free email account with 5GB of storage for documents, mail, photos and videos, and backups. Well, the good news is that the purchased Apps don't count in the available space.

i.   Sign in with your Apple ID:

If you forgot to sign in during the set-up, follow these steps:

- Go to settings.
- Select sign in to your iPhone.
- Enter the previous Apple ID and password or create one if you don't possess an Apple ID.
- For the protection with two-factor authentication, you'll have to enter the six-digit code.

- Changing Apple ID Settings:
  - Go to Settings > [your name].

- You'll have the following options.

    - Update your contact information.

    - Change your password.

    - Manage family sharing.

- iCloud Settings:

  - Go to Settings > [your name] > iCloud.

  - You can do the following:

    - View your iCloud storage.

    - Upgrade it, select manage storage > Change storage plan.

    - Switch on the desired features such as Photos, Mail, Messages, and Contacts.

- Different Uses of iCloud on the iPhone:

  You can keep the following updated while using iCloud:

  - Photos and Videos.

    - Uploading photos and videos on iCloud allows you access to them from any device in which you're signed in with your Apple

ID. Also, the photos and videos stored in the iCloud are always in full resolution, saving up space in your iPhone's internal storage. (Note: to get access to photos and videos your device must have iOS 8.1, or it should be iPadOS 13, OS X 10.10.3, or a PC with iCloud for Windows 7.)

- To switch on the iCloud photos, Go to Settings > [your name] > iCloud > photos, and then turn on iCloud Photos.

- The videos and photos are automatically stored in iCloud because Optimize iPhone Storage is turned on by default. To switch it off Go to Settings > [your name] > iCloud > Photos, and then select Optimize iCloud Storage.

- You can share photos and videos anywhere in full resolution. Simply choose a photo or video from your library, select edit, and then tap cancel. The video or photo starts downloading on its own in full resolution.

- Tap on this⬆️, and then select a device that you want to share your data with.

- The iCloud storage plan can also be upgraded in case of exceeding your storage plan; Go to settings > [your name] > iCloud > Manage Storage > Change storage plan.

- Documents

  - To set up the drive on the iCloud, Go to Settings > [your name] > iCloud, and then switch on iCloud Drive

  - Browsing an iCloud drive is very handy, go to the browser located at the bottom of the screen, under locations, tap iCloud Drive, and select a folder to open it.

  - You can also select the specific apps to use the iCloud drive, go to settings > [your name] > iCloud, and then simply switch on or off each of the Apps present in the list under iCloud drive.

- Contacts, Mail, Calendars, Messages, Notes, and Reminders.

- Music, Books, and Apps.

- Passwords and credit card details. (These can also be available on your other devices using the iCloud keychain.)

- Bookmarks, webpages you have browsed in Safari, and your reading list.

- You can also locate easily your iPhone with iCloud if it's lost.

- View your iCloud's data on other Apple devices.

- Share conveniently your photos and videos.

- Restore your data and get it backed up.

- Share location with your friends and family; you all can share it. Follow each other on the map.

- **Setting up Face ID and Apple pay:**

  Face ID is said to be the safest way for the security of your iPhone, it should be set up at the time of setting up the phone. Also, it's known to be the quickest way to get into the phone; however, the Face ID setup is also very easy, a setup will pop up on your screen after going to Settings > Face ID and Passcode > Set Up Face ID and will ask you to turn your face a couple of times in different directions and then once your face is recognized; your privacy is guaranteed. Apple doesn't let it go to any third party, your photos and videos and everything is always kept safe within your iPhone, not even Apple takes it.

- To temporarily disable the Face ID you can press and keep pressed the side button and any volume button for 2 seconds, after the appearance of sliders, immediately press the side button to lock it automatically, if you do not continue holding the button, the iPhone remains locked until reopened by entering the pin, which also enables the Face ID again.

- To switch it off completely follow: Settings > Face ID and Passcode

  - Switch off the Face ID for specific items, including Phone Unlock, Apple Pay, App Store, and iTunes, or Safari Autofill.

Apple Pay is only possible to set up when the Face ID is activated on the iPhone. You'll simply have to follow the on-screen instructions in Apple's wallet to set your Apple Pay. Also, Apple doesn't allow the new iPhone to extract the previously saved information of credit cards, for obvious security reasons, you'll have to re-enter every card detail on Apple Pay.

Learning initial things:

a. Home screen and lock-screen:

Here is a detailed guide for you to learn everything about the home screen and the lock screen.

- Waking up and unlocking the iPhone:

As the iPhone turns the screen black when not in use to save the battery's life, to secure it, and for safety, goes to sleep automatically while not being used. To wake up the phone again, follow these steps:

- Press the side sleep/wake button.

- It can simply be awakened by raising the iPhone, but this feature can also be turned off by Going to Settings > Display & Brightness.

- Double tapping on the screen also awakens it.

Unlocking an iPhone with Face ID is a simple and the quickest way to enter the phone:

- Tap the screen or raise your iPhone 12 Pro Max, and then look at your iPhone. The lock icon will swiftly shift from closed to open, indicating that the phone is unlocked.

- Swiping up from the bottom of the screen is another way of unlocking, you may be asked to enter a passcode if face ID somehow fails to recognize you.

Unlocking an iPhone 12 Pro Max with Passcode is also simple:

To set up the passcode first, if you haven't already, Go to Settings > Tap Face ID and Passcode, and then set a passcode by turning passcode on or with Change passcode. To see options for setting a password, open Passcode Options. (Note: it's better to use Custom Alphanumeric Codes and Custom Numeric Codes for more security.)

Setting up the passcode is always a safe option because when wearing a mask or out in public, the iPhone may not be able to recognize you and you may be unable to log in to your iPhone 12 Pro Max using the Face ID. In that situation, you can also open it using the passcode. Also enabling a passcode turns on data protection automatically, by which the encryption of your iPhone data is done with the 256-bit AES encryption.

- Change iPhone's lock-screen timings:

To change the timings of auto-locking in iPhone, Go to Settings > Display and Brightness > Auto-lock, then choose a length of time.

- Multiple Attempts setting:

In order to set the iPhone to erase all data when the wrong passcode is entered more than ten times, Go to Settings > Face ID and Passcode > Switch on Erase Data. (Note: After removal of the data, you will have to restore your device from a set backup and then set your device again as a new.

- Switch off Passcode:

You can turn off Passcode by Going to Settings > Face ID and Passcode > Turn Passcode off.

- Reset the Passcode:

If in case, you have forgotten your passcode the recovery mode or your computer can be used to erase all your data and then set up a new passcode. The iPhone gets disabled after you enter your passcode wrongly six times and you get locked out of your device. (If you had been cautious enough to have created a backup on the iCloud or your computer, you'll be able to recover your data and settings from it later.)

To unlock iPhone 12 Pro Max using the Passcode, you'll simply have to swipe up from the bottom of the lock-screen and then enter the Passcode in the bar that pops up.

- Learn different gestures:

There are so many different gestures on your new iPhone 12 Pro Max:

- To go back to the **home screen** after using an App or at any time; you can just swipe up on the screen from the bottom.

  - You can also open Apps on the home screen; swipe left to right to scroll through the Apps. By tapping on the App's icon, you can open it. To return to the home screen, slide up from the bottom of the screen.

  - To access your widgets, slide right on the first home screen, find the edit button for this by simply dragging it down. You can edit this to deliver the precise info that you desire to see.

- To access the **controls quickly**, you can swipe down from the top-right corner; it'll open up the control center, from it you can select the control and keep holding it to reveal various options. For addition and removal of a control Go to Settings > Control Center.

  Here's how to use the control center:

  - After opening the control center as it gives quick access to many useful controls such as Apps, airplane mode, do not disturb, volume, screen brightness, and a flashlight. You can do the following things:

a) The several options in the controls can be accessed by tapping on them and then holding them. Tap and hold the top-left group of controls, and then tap⊚, the AirDrop options open up.

b) Tap and hold 🖸 to access camera features like taking selfies, recording videos, etc.

- The control center can also be customized by adding shortcuts of Apps or controls to it. You can do it by following these steps:

a) Go to settings > Control center

b) For the addition of a control tap ⊕, for the removal tap ⊖ present right next to them.

c) For rearrangement of controls, tap ≡ right beside the control. By this, you can drag it to whatever position you like.

- You can temporarily disconnect and reconnect the Wi-Fi in Control Center tap 📶. You can also view the name of the connected Wi-Fi network, select and hold 📶. (Note: in this way, the Wi-Fi isn't turned off as you just disconnected it from a network, AirPlay and AirDrop are still working and iPhone connects to the known networks automatically as you restart it or change your location. To switch it off, go to Settings > Wi-Fi. To switch it on again tap 📶.)

- You can temporarily connect and disconnect from the Bluetooth devices as well by simply tapping 🔵 in the control center. (Note: in this way the Bluetooth is just disconnected from the devices which allow other services and location accuracy to stay on. To switch off the Bluetooth, you'll have to go to Settings > Bluetooth, and then to switch it on again you'll have to just tap 🔵.)

- To switch off the access to the control center in apps, go to Settings > Control Center, and then tap turn off access within apps.

- To access the **App Switcher**, put your finger at the bottom of the screen and while sliding it upwards stop in the middle of the screen, lift your finger. You can browse the opened Apps by swiping right, and then choosing the desired App.

- You can also **switch between the open Apps** by sliding right or left with your finger at the bottom of the screen.

- To **quickly turn off the Apps**, you can force kill the Apps as well by tapping at the bottom of the screen and then swiping up slightly but don't leave the screen immediately. This will return you to the home screen, then lift your finger. By swiping up on any app card, it will close it forcefully.

- To activate **Siri** just say "Hey Siri" or keep pressing the side button, and then say whatever you want. Siri will listen until you leave the button.

- To use **Apple Pay,** press the side button twice, your default credit card will be revealed, and then look at the iPhone for authentication with the Face ID.

- You can use **Accessibility shortcuts** by pressing the side button thrice.

- To take a **screenshot,** click and release the power/side button and volume up button simultaneously. Tap the screenshot present in the lower-left corner, and then tap done. Select Save to Photos, Save to Files, or Delete Screenshot. To create a screen recording Go to Settings > Control Center, then tap/present next to sound recording. After it, open Control Center and then tap⊙, the recording will begin after 3 seconds count down. To stop it, open the control center, tap ⊙ or a red-colored status bar showing at the top of the screen, tap stop. You can go to Photos and choose your recording.

- To use **Emergency SOS** (in every country and region except India), click the side button and either volume button together until the sliders drop-down, then drag emergency SOS.

- There is a slightly different way to use **Emergency SOS in India**, press the side-button thrice, if the accessibility shortcut is turned on, click and hold the side button and either volume button until the sliders become visible, and then simply drag the Emergency SOS.

- To **Turn iPhone off** click and hold the side button and either volume button until the slider becomes visible, then slide the power off slider. You can also Go to Settings > General > Shut Down. To turn iPhone on, simply click and hold the side button until the Apple logo becomes visible on the screen.

- You can **Force Restart** your iPhone by pressing and releasing the volume up button and then pressing and releasing the volume down button, and then pressing and holding the side button until the Apple logo becomes visible on the screen.

- *Volume adjustments:*

The volume of the songs, movies, or other media is adjusted when you're on your phone or listening to or watching something by pressing the side buttons present on the iPhone. While these buttons are used to adjust the volume for alerts, calls, or other sound effects; Siri also helps in volume adjustments.

- You can set up Siri, by going to Settings > Siri & Search, if you want to ask Siri by your voice; you'll have to switch on Listen for "Hey Siri", summoning Siri with a button is made possible by turning on "Press Side Button for Siri".

You can just say "Hey Siri, turn up the volume" or you can say "Hey Siri, turn the volume down"

- You can lock the alert volumes and ringer also by going to settings > tap sounds and haptics, and then switch off with buttons.

- You can adjust the volume in the control center. Tap control center, and   drag   ).

- The headphone volume can be limited to protect your ears. To do that, go to Settings > Sounds and haptics > Headphone Safety, switch on Reduce Loud Sounds, then slide the slider for the selection of maximum decibel level for headphone sound. (Tip: you can also stop changes to the maximum headphone audio by screen time turned on. Go to Settings > Screen Time > Content and Privacy

Restrictions > Reduce Loud Sounds, and then choose Don't Allow.)

- Calls, notifications, and alerts can be temporarily silenced by opening the control center, and then tap☾.

- iPhone can be put on silent☓ or ring ⌂ mode, turn over silent/ring; switch present at the side. (Note: the ring mode lets iPhone play all the sounds while the silent mode turns the light orange and doesn't let iPhone play any alert or sound, but it will still vibrate and music, games, clock alarms play sounds through their built-in speaker even when the silent/ring mode is set to silent. Also, in some regions or countries, Emergency alerts and Memos are played, when iPhone is in silent mode.

- Modifying Sounds and Vibrations:

You can choose the sounds iPhone selects to play for calls, texts, voicemails, reminders, emails, or other notifications. You will feel a tap, which is known as Haptic Feedback, after performing a few actions example, tapping and holding the camera icon on the home screen.

- You can set vibration and sound options by Going to Settings > Sounds and Haptics and then you can do the following:

    - For setting up the tones and vibration patterns for audio, tap a sound type, for example, text tone or ringtone.

    - For setting up the volume for every type of sound, slide the slider below Alerts and Ringers.

    - You can select a tone, scroll to view it. (Note: ringtones are for the alarms, calls, and clock timer, while text tones are played for new messages, alerts, new voice mails, etc.)

    - Tap vibration, select a vibration pattern, or you can create your vibration by tapping on Create New Vibration.

- You switch Haptic Feedbacks on or off by going to Settings > Sounds and haptics > Switch Haptics and Sounds on or off. (When System Haptics are turned off, the vibrations will not be heard or felt by you for incoming alerts and calls, also if in case the calls and vibrations aren't being heard or felt even when it is turned on, then Go to Control center and check if Do not Disturb is switched on, if the icon ☾ is highlighted then it means that the Do not disturb is turned on, tap it to turn it off, also note that when Do not Disturb is switched on, ☾ is visible on the notification/status bar as well.)

- ***Opening App Library and Changing common settings:***

There's a settings app in the app library or your home screen, tap on it to open up the settings and change the important ones, for example, notification sounds, and your passcode, etc.

- Tap Settings.
- Swipe from the top of the search bar; enter words, for example, "iTunes", then select the setting.

You can also adjust colors and screen brightness on iPhone; to save battery life it's best to dim the screen, set Dark Mode, and apply Night Shift, you can adjust your screen for the conditions of lightning automatically.

The dark mode is used for a different experience while using the iPhone, it's best for dim light environments. It can be turned on in the control center or set to turn on at night automatically by a custom schedule in settings. The advantage of using Dark mode is that at night it won't disturb those around you while you can still use your phone.

To switch on or off **Dark Mode**:

- You can either; Go to Control Center > press and keep pressed ☀, and then tap ◑ to switch the Dark Mode on or off.
- Or you can Go to settings > Display and Brightness > Choose Dark to switch on Dark Mode or choose Light to switch it off.

To set **Dark Mode** to switch on or off automatically:

- Go to Settings > Display and Brightness > Turn on Automatic, and then tap options.
- You'll get two options to choose from, Sunset to Sunrise, or Custom Schedule. (Note: by choosing Custom Schedule, you can tap the options to set schedule timings

to turn Dark Mode off and on. (If you choose Sunset to Sunrise option, the data from your clock and location will be used by iPhone to determine your nighttime.)

You can either **adjust the screen brightness by yourself** every time:

- Go to Control Centre, and then drag the icon.
- Go to Settings > Display and brightness and then slide the slider.

Or you can **set it to adjust automatically**:

- For the adjustment of light according to the environmental light; the iPhone uses a built-in ambient light sensor, or its activation Go to Settings > Accessibility > Display and Text Size, and then switch on Auto-Brightness.

You can **switch True Tone** off or on; while turned on, it can fetch the color and intensity of the display, matching with the environmental light. To turn it on, follow the steps below:

- Simply Go to Control Center > press the button with the sun symbol ☀, and then tap ☀ to switch True Tone on or off.

- Or you can do it by going to settings > Display and Brightness, and then switch True Tone off or on.

You can **Switch Night Shift off or on:**

It is used mostly in the shifting of colors in the display from bright to warm in order to ease the viewing of the screen on eyes at night.

It can be done manually by:

- Go to Control Center > tap and hold ☀, and then tap ☀.

It can also be set to turn on or off automatically by:

- Go to Settings > Display and Brightness > Night Shift.

- Switch on scheduled.

- For the adjustment of color balancing for Night Shift, slide the slider from the low color temperature position towards the warmer or cooler end of the spectrum.

- Tap From, "select from Sunset to Sunrise, or Custom Schedule". (Note: if you choose a custom schedule, you can easily select options for scheduling when to turn on or off the Night Shift. Or if you choose Sunset to Sunrise, then iPhone will use your location and clock timings for the determination of nighttime. Also, Sunset to Sunrise doesn't work when the location service is switched off in the settings. You can turn this on by going to Settings > Privacy, or if the Setting Time Zone is switched off; go to Settings > Privacy > Location Service > System Services.

The **screen can be magnified with Display zoom in iPhone 12 Pro Max** by going to settings > Display and Brightness, tap view (under Display Zoom) select zoomed and then set.

The iPhone's name is used by iCloud, Personal Hotspot, AirDrop, and PC, you can change it by going to settings > General > About > Name, then just tap ⊗, enter a new name, and then tap done.

Date and Time can either be set automatically by going to settings > General > Date and Time, and then switching on Set automatically (Note: The correct date and time is fetched by iPhone over the networks, but as some networks don't provide network time, therefore in some regions and countries, iPhone doesn't detect and set it automatically.

Or

You can also select the **24-Hour time,** by going to settings > General > Date and Time and then select 24 Hour Time in which iPhone displays time from 0 to 23 hours.

To set your **region and language** if you haven't set it already during the setup, you can do it after moving to a new place or while traveling by going to Settings > General > Language and Region, you will have the options to set:

- Your region.
- Preferred language.
- The format of the calendar.
- Temperature unit (Fahrenheit or Celsius).

The other **keyboard and language can be added** by tapping Add language, then choose a language. Many typing features can be turned on or off, like, spell checking; adding another keyboard for the text in other languages, and also the layout of your keyboards; both wireless and onscreen can be changed. (Note: after adding another keyboard, you can easily write in two languages without having to switch between them continuously as it will automatically switch between the two most often used languages or keyboards.) For the **addition or removal of another keyboard,** go to settings > General > Keyboard, then tap keyboards and you'll have the following options:

- Add a new keyboard: select add a new keyboard, and then just select a keyboard from the appeared list. For the addition of more keyboards, repeat the step.

- To remove a new keyboard: select edit, tap ⊖present right beside the keyboard you want to delete, tap delete, and then tap done.

- To reorder your keyboard list: tap edit, drag ≡ icon located beside the keyboard to allot it a new place in the list, then tap done. (Note: after the addition of different languages' keyboards, the new language is automatically added to the languages on the order list of preferences of languages.) You can see it and add other languages directly by going to the settings > general > language and region.

The list can also be reordered to change the display of text in apps and websites.

You can switch to a new keyboard by doing:

- Tapping and holding 😊 or 🌐.
- Then tap on the name of the keyboard you want to get switched to.

And you can just tap 😊or 🌐 to switch to another keyboard, if you continue tapping it will give you access to other enabled keyboards.

You can **switch to the magic keyboard from the language keyboard**. (Note: Magic keyboard has a numeric keypad to enter text on the iPhone, it connects to iPhone using Bluetooth, powered by the built-in rechargeable battery.) (It is sold separately.)

Pairing the magic keyboard with an iPhone is easy, firstly be assured that it is charged, and then it is done by going to Settings > Bluetooth, switch it on, and then choose the device from the other devices list. (If already paired with other devices, the magic keyboard won't work unless it is unpaired from the other devices, then it'll be able to connect to your iPhone.)

Reconnecting iPhone to the Magic keyboard is easy; when you switch it off or go out of reach of the Bluetooth device; it disconnects itself. You can reconnect it by turning the switch on or getting back into the range of the Bluetooth and tapping any key. (Note: when connected with the magic keyboard, the other keyboard doesn't appear.)

Switching to the onscreen keyboard to avoid the usage of an external keyboard to perform other actions is also easy, you have to first view the onscreen keyboard, and then tap ⏏ on the external keyboard. To hide it back tap ⏏ again.

 To switch to the emoji keyboard from the language keyboard and vice versa, press and hold the control key on the magic keyboard. Tap and hold the spacebar to switch between emoji, any other language keyboard, and English.

You **can open search in the magic keyboard** by tapping the Command - space.

Typing options for the Magic keyboard can also be changed, which includes the iPhone's response to an external keyboard typing. You can do it by going to settings > General > Keyboard > Hardware Keyboard and then you'll have the following options:

- You can **assign an alternative** keyboard layout by tapping a language at the top of the screen, and then selecting an alternative layout present in the list.

- You can **switch Auto-capitalization off or on**. While selecting this option in the supported apps, the iPhone automatically capitalizes the first word and proper nouns.

- You can also **switch Auto-correction off or** on. When this is selected, all the apps supported by this feature automatically correct the spelling mistakes.

- You can **switch "." Shortcut off or on**, after selecting this option, a double tap on the space bar will insert a period.

- **The command key or other modifier keys' actions can be changed** by tapping Modifier keys; tapping a key and then choosing an action you wish to be performed by it.

For **assigning an alternative layout to the keyboard** go to Settings > General > Keyboard > Keyboards, then tap a language at the top of the screen, then choose an alternative layout.

Apart from iPhone working with the apps that come with it, iCloud is also able to work with Microsoft Exchange and many of the highly popular internet-based contacts, emails, and calendar services. **For setting up the mail account** go to Settings > Mail > Accounts > Add Account then you will have the following two options:

- Either you tap on an email service, for instance, iCloud, and then simply enter your email information.

Or

- You can tap other, tap "Add Mail Account", and then enter your information for setting up a new account.

For setting a contact's account go to Settings > Contacts > Accounts > Add Account > Other, and then tap LDAP Account or CardDAV Account, and then enter your server and account information.

For setting up a calendar account go to Settings > Calendar > Accounts > Add Account tap other; you'll then have the following options:

- You can tap on Add a Calendar account, and then just tap Add CalDAV Account; your account, and server information.

Or

- You subscribe to iCal (.ics) Calendars: Tap Add Subscribed Calendar, and then enter the URL of the .ics file to subscribe to; or it can also be imported.

- Lock screen and quick access to features:

A lot of features such as the camera, control center, can be accessed through the lock screen. You can also get information from your preferred apps quickly and can view notifications.

You can do the following actions:

- To open the camera; just swipe left. Moreover, in the iPhone 12 Pro Max, you can tap and hold and then leave it.

- To open the control center; swipe down from the top-right edge.

- To see earlier/previous notifications; just swipe upward from the center.

- You can view today's view by swiping right.

To **select the apps that you want to see on the lock screen;** there is an option by going to Settings > Face ID and Passcode; you'll get the following options:

By turning the access to these off or on you'll prevent or allow some useful features to appear or disappear while the iPhone is locked.

- Notification Center.

- Widgets.

- Siri.

- Control Center.

- Replying to messages.

- Returning missed calls

- Wallet.

- Home control.

- Connecting to Windows, PC, Mac, or an object with USB (note that after changing the default setting and allowing the USB to connect with your iPhone; when it is locked, you'll put your iPhone at a risk).

- Also, you can give your emergency contacts and medical information in a Medical ID that anyone can view even when your iPhone is locked.

You can **show previews of the notifications on the lock screen** by going to Settings > Notifications, tap previews, and then tap always. It will show lines from mail messages, texts from messages, and calendar invitation details.

- How to open apps and explore the App Library:

All of your apps are shown on your home screen in the form of organized pages; if you want to add more apps more pages will be given. Also, these apps can be accessed in-app library, which is available at the end of the home screen pages where all the apps are located in an organized and easy to access view.

To **Open Apps on the Home Screen:** firstly, go to the home screen by swiping up from the bottom corner of the screen. By swiping left or right on the home screen you'll browse the apps. To open a particular app, tap on its icon, and then for returning to the first page swipe up from the bottom corner of the screen.

In an **App library,** the apps are sorted in their respective categories, like Entertainment, Social, Creativity, etc. In it, you'll have the following options and you can do them by:

- Simply open an app, tap on its icon.
- Search for the app, tap the search field given at the top of the screen, where apps are listed alphabetically, or you can just enter the name of the app.
- You can perform instant actions by tapping and holding an app to open its quick actions menu. (Note: if kept hold, the quick action, and menu, and no action is selected it will result in the automatic jiggling of the icons. You'll then have to tap done before trying again.)
- Press and keep pressed the app to open a quick actions menu, and then select Add to Home screen. If it's unavailable on the home screen, the app is still shown in the app library, in this way; an app is added to the home screen.

- Deleting an app from the iPhone 12 Pro Max is also easy by tapping and holding the app, select delete app, then tap delete. In this way, the app is deleted from both the app library and the home screen.

- To add new apps from the app store to the library or the home screen or just to the library, go to Settings > Home Screen, and then you can either add it to the library only or add it to the home screen.

You can **show and hide Home Screen pages** for your convenience, to do this, put the app library closer to the first home screen page by tapping and holding the app on the home screen, then tap edit home screen, until the apps begin to jiggle, then tap the dots present at the home screen (as seen the thumbnail images have checkmarks below them). Tap these checkmarks to hide pages and to show the hidden pages; tap to add the checkmarks and then tap done two times.

- Taking screenshots and doing screen recording:

You can **take a screenshot** (which means taking a picture of the screen from top to bottom) by doing the following:

- Simultaneously pressing and then releasing the power/home button and volume up button.

- Then select the screenshot in the lower-left corner and then choose done.

- You'll have three options: save to files, photos, or delete them. After choosing 'save to photos', it can be viewed in the screenshot folder in the photos or if iCloud photos are turned on, then it can also be shown in the all photos album by going to settings > photos. (Note: you can create a pdf file by tapping on the thumbnail after taking the screenshot and then tapping full page.)

You can do screen recording and capture sound on your iPhone 12 Pro Max by going to Settings > Control center, tap ⊕ located beside the screen recording, open control center, then tap ⊙. After waiting for a three-second countdown, the recording will begin. To stop it, open again the control center, select ⊙ or the status bar at the top of the screen, tap stop.

You can find it in the screen recording in the photos.

- Choosing new wallpaper:

You can either select an image (dynamic or still), or the default wallpapers for the lock screen or home screen by going to Settings > Wallpaper > Select a new wallpaper.

Then you can do any of the following:

- You can select a preset image (still, dynamic, etc.) from a group present at the top of the screen. (Note: when dark mode is turned on, wallpapers with ◐ change their appearances.)

- You can also choose one of your pictures by tapping an album and then selecting the photo. (To change the position of your selected image you can pinch it outward to zoom, and it can be dragged by your finger, and then pinch it closed to zoom out.)

- You can turn on perceptive zoom, not available with all wallpaper choices, by tapping ⤢, which is a cool feature that lets your wallpaper move along with the viewing angle. (It is to note that it doesn't appear if the 'Reduce motion' is switched on in the settings > accessibility > motion.)

Then by tapping set, three options will appear, select any of the following:

- Set Home Screen.
- Set Lock Screen.
- Set both.

(Note: for the already set wallpaper, perceptive zoom can be opened by going to Settings > Wallpaper, tapping the image of the lock screen or home screen, and then tapping Perceptive Zoom.)

To **select a live photo as your lock screen wallpaper**, go to settings > wallpaper > choose a new wallpaper. Then you'll have two options:

- Tapping live, and then selecting a live photo.
- Tapping the live photos album, then selecting a live photo (it may be downloaded).

After it, you can tap the set, and then select your option from the set as lock screen or both.

- Increasing reachability:

To increase the reachability of the items by bringing them to the home screen, go to Settings > Accessibility > tap, and then switch on the reachability. Bringing the top of the screen is done by swiping down on the bottom corner of the screen. The screen can be reset by tapping the top of the screen.

- Using app switcher:

All of your open apps can be seen in the app switch by swiping up from the bottom corner of the screen and stop in the middle of the screen. For browsing the open apps, swipe right, and then tap the app you wish to open.

You **can quickly switch between open apps** by swiping right or left at the bottom corner of the screen.

- The picture-in-picture feature:

You can use other apps while doing FaceTime or watching a video. To activate it while watching a video or doing FaceTime, just tap on . The window shrinks down to any corner of your screen and the home screen appears for you to choose other apps. Along with the video screen, you'll have the following:

- Pinch open the video screen to enlarge its size and then pinch it closed to shrink back to the small window.

- Moving the video window is done by dragging it to a different edge of the screen.

- You can tap ⊗ to lose the window.

- The controls can be hidden and shown by tapping the video window.

- To go back to the full screen of video or FaceTime tap

- Moving apps:

To move apps on the home screen, tap and hold it, then after tapping 'Edit Home Screen', the jiggling of apps begins. You can drag it to any location like:

- New location on the same page.

- The dock present at the bottom of the screen.

- New or different home screen page.

And then tap done.

- Organizing apps:

The groups can be created, and folders are made by tapping and holding the app's icon present on the home screen, then tapping "Edit Home Screen"; the jiggling of apps begins. To make a folder, drag it onto the other app and can similarly drag other apps to the same folder.

You can rename an app by tapping on the name field, and then putting in a new name. When it is finished, tap done. (Note: the folder can be deleted by moving all the apps out of it.)

You can reset the apps and home screen back to their original positions by going to Settings > General > Reset, and then tap reset home screen layout. The folders are deleted after that, and the newly downloaded apps are arranged alphabetically after the iPhone's app.

- If an app isn't working:

If an app is temporarily crashed, you can shut it and then reopen it; to improve its working by opening the app switcher and then swiping right to find it and then swiping it up. To reopen it, go back to the app library or home screen and then tap on it to open it up. (Note: if it still doesn't start working; try restarting your iPhone.)

- Deleting the apps:

To delete an app from the home screen, tap and keep taped its icon until the quick action's menu becomes visible, and then tap delete an app. If you want to keep it in the app library; select "Move to app library" and then select remove the app.

Various apps can also be removed besides the external downloaded apps such as:

- Calendar.
- Compass.
- Calculator.
- Books.
- FaceTime.
- Mail.
- iTunes.
- Home.
- Files.
- Maps.

- Measure.

- Music.

- News.

- Podcasts.

- Notes.

- Reminders.

- Voice memos.

- Watch.

- Shortcuts.

- Stocks.

- Tips.

- Translate.

- Watch.

- Weather.

- TV.

xi.   How to dictate text:

You can switch on the dictation by going to settings > general > keyboard and then switch on "Enable dictation". To start dictating, text tap 🎤 on the keyboard, when you are through with talking tap ⌨. The text can be replaced and entered by dictating; simply tap on the insertion point, and then tap 🎤. You can add punctuated text by speaking the punctuation marks, like a comma, dot, dollar sign, period, quote and end quote, question mark, new paragraph, new line, colon, semicolon, all caps (for making the next word all upper case), no space, hashtag, smiley, frowny, winky (to add emojis), exclamation point, open and close parenthesis.

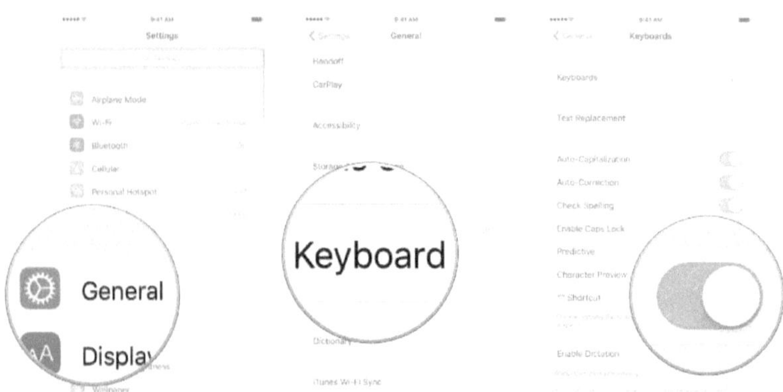

xii.   Searching with iPhone:

iPhone gives in-app search as well as searching for the app themselves. It will also open and find appropriate web pages according to the search. You can choose the apps to search with by going to Settings >Siri and search and then scrolling down, tapping an app, then turning "Show in search" on or off. To search with an iPhone swipe down from the center of the home screen, tap the searching field, then enter what you want to search; you will have the following options:

- Make the keyboard invisible and view more results on the screen by tapping go.
- Tapping on the suggested tab to open it.
- To do a new search, tap ⊗ and then enter the new text.

You can also turn off suggestions in the search by going to settings > Siri and Search, and then switch off suggestions in search.

The location services can be turned off for suggestions by going to settings > privacy > location services, then tap system services, and then switch off location-based suggestions.

Dictionaries can be added to help in search by going to settings > general > dictionary and then choose a dictionary.

xiii.   Sharing items:

You can share items using AirDrop by opening the item, then tapping ⬆, share, AirDrop, •••, or the button the app uses as a sharing option, then tapping ⦿ present in the row of share options, and then tapping the profile picture of an AirDrop user that is nearby. (Note: on your iPhone 12 Pro Max you can also do it by pointing your iPhone in the direction of another iPhone 11 models or iPhone 12 models, and then tap the user's profile picture shown at the top of the screen).

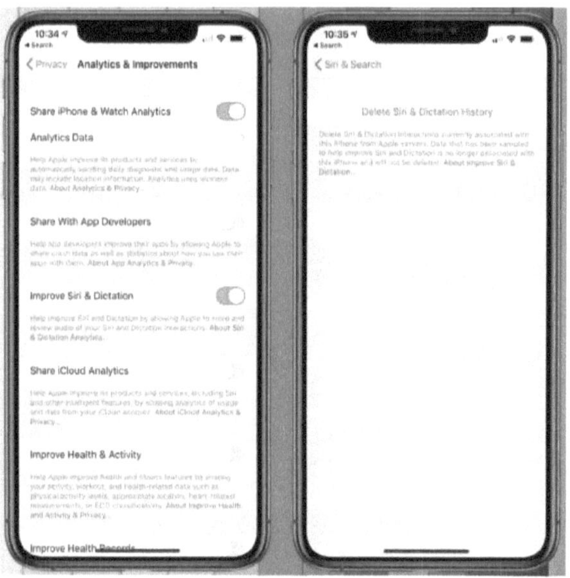

If the device doesn't appear as a nearby AirDrop user, then AirDrop should be allowed to receive items in the control center of their phone. Items can also be shared by other options like mails and messages. Also, a few different options might be suggested to you by Siri, showing the profile pictures of the users along with their sharing methods.

You can also let others send items to you via AirDrop by going to settings > and then tapping ⓘ if it appears, if not, then by tapping and holding the top-left of the controls. Then you can either select contacts only or everyone to choose the person you want to receive items from. The options for accepting and declining will appear before every item.

xiv.   Shortcuts and performing quick actions

The quick actions menu can be opened by tapping and holding the apps to open the quick actions menu.

- Tapping and holding a camera will open up many options and you can select take selfies for instance.
- Tapping and holding maps and selecting send my location is another example.

Tapping and holding an icon for too long will make all the apps jiggle so tap done after it.

Similarly, you can do the following:

- Tapping and holding an image in the photos will make visible a list of options to choose from.

- Tapping and holding a message in the mail will make visible the contents of the message and a list of options.

- Tapping and holding any item in the control center like a camera will put before you a list of options.

- Tapping and holding a notification on the lock screen for a quick response.

- Tapping and holding the space bar, while typing will make your keyboard a trackpad.

xv.   Addition of widgets to the home screen:

You can **add so many widgets** for your convenience to **the home screen** in order to make it easier for you to get access to the basic information. You can move them from today's view by opening today's view and by swiping right from the left corner of the home screen or the lock screen, and then scrolling and searching for the widget. After finding it, keep tapping and holding it until the jiggling begins, then slide it off the right side; you'll be back to the home screen from where you can now put it in a place you'd like and then tap done. (Note: smart stack has all the widgets organized by using the time, location, and activity and thus it displays the most relevant widget at the time of need. It can be added to the home screen and can be swiped by to locate the widget you want.

To add the widget to the home screen, go to the home screen page where you wish it to be added, then press the home screen background until the jiggling of the apps begins. Tap + present at the top of the screen, it opens the widget gallery. After finding the widget you wish to add, tap it, and then swipe all the way right through the size options; after finding the desired size, tap "Add widget" and then tap done.

Widgets can be customized by tapping and holding a widget to open the quick actions menu on the home screen. Tap "Edit widget" or "Edit stack", then select options, and after it; tap on your home screen.

Removing a widget from the home screen is done by tapping and holding the widget to browse the quick actions menu, and then tapping "Remove Widget" or "Remove stack", then tap Remove.

Today's view can also be allowed to get access to when the iPhone is locked by going to Settings > Face ID and Passcode, and then enter your passcode, switch on "Today view" under Allow Access when locked.

xvi.   Learn all about the iPhone's battery:

Firstly, learn how to charge your iPhone's battery; you can do it by connecting to a power outlet with the help of a charging cable, and Apple's USB power adapter.

To **check the percentage of the remaining battery** you can swipe down from the top-right corner.

The **low power mode can be turned on** by going to settings > battery, and then turning on low power mode; it will increase the usage time of the battery. Also, if switched to low power mode automatically; the iPhone will go back to normal power mode when the charging is 80%.

You can check the performance of your battery usage by going to settings > battery

Learn what does your activity means:

- Last charge level: shows the last time when the battery was fully charged and the time of disconnection.

- Activity by the app: indicates the total time the app was being used.

- Battery usage by the app: the usage of battery by each app at a particular time by each app is shown in this.

- The screen on and screen off: total time and activity in it when the screen was turned off or on and the average for the last 10 days will also be shown.

- Battery usage graph: shows the exact percentage of battery usage every day.

- Activity graph: it indicates all the activities with the time.

- Battery level graph: it shows charging intervals, battery level, and time when the battery was critically low, or Apple entered lower power mode.

- Insights and suggestions: the insights of the usage patterns that might have caused the iPhone to use energy, there will also be suggestions to lower the battery consumption be shown to you.

Checking your battery's health is easy by going to settings > battery, and then tapping battery health.

Optimization of battery charging is done by going to settings > battery, tapping battery health, switch on Optimized battery charging.

xvii.   Traveling with the iPhone 12 Pro Max:

While traveling you can turn on airplane mode by opening the control center and tapping ✈. It can also be turned on by going to settings, where if it is already turned one then ✈ is shown. Turning on Wi-Fi or Bluetooth, while airplane mode is also turned on, is done by opening the control center, then tapping 🛜 to turn on Wi-Fi, ✳ this to turn Bluetooth on.

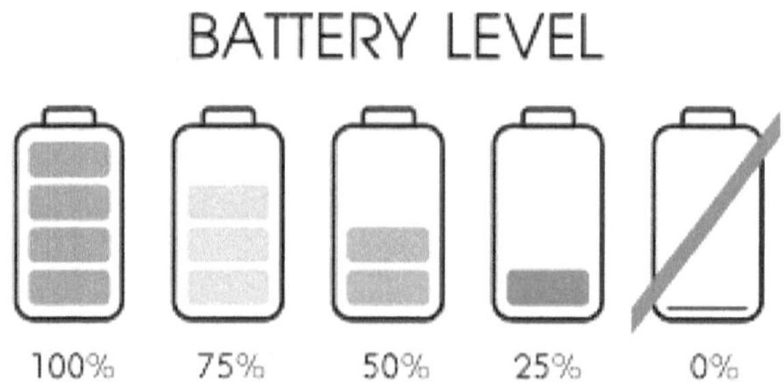

Part 2

INTO THE PHONE

Chapter 2

Basic Apps and Features:

a. From the store:

You **can get apps from the store,** but you'll need an Apple ID and an internet connection to get access to the apps in the store. You can get apps by asking Siri, for instance, you can say "Search the app store for novels apps" or you can tap on any of these:

- Search: enter text and then tap search.

- Today: it shows featured stories.

- Apps: in it, you can find new releases, or browse by category or you can view top charts.

You can **see more information about apps** like:

- Size of the file.

- Previews or screenshots.

- Reviews and ratings.

- Privacy information.

- Languages supported by it.

- Compatibility with Apple devices.

- Family sharing support and game center.

If you **want to download an app** and you see, ☁ then it means you have bought it and you can download it once again without paying. If an app is free you can tap "Get it to download"; if you want to buy it, then verify first using, your Face ID or passcode.

Sharing an app is easy by tapping on the app's icon to know more details and then tapping ⬆ after it, selecting a sharing option or a gift card.

Subscribing to apple arcade is also easy you can go to the app store, select arcade, and then either you can start a free one-month subscription or start a monthly subscription, and then after a confirmation with the Face ID you'll get subscribed to any of them. If you want to unsubscribe, simply go to the app store, tap ⊙ or the profile picture, and then tap subscriptions, and then tap apple arcade click on unsubscribe. (Note: after you unsubscribe; the downloaded games won't be played.)

The **app clips** are there for quick access to the apps without needing to download them; you can find and use an app click after discovering one by tapping the app clip link in the safari, messages, or maps, or by bringing your iPhone close to the NFC (near-field communication) tag. For the removal of app clips, go to settings > app clips and then tap Remove All App Clips.

You can also discover and download games by tapping:

- Search: Search for the game you're looking for.
- Games: you can find new releases, view top charts, and search by categories.
- Arcade: find games in the apple arcade

You can buy them by tapping the price or by tapping "Get" for free games. You can also **play games with anyone using game center** by going to settings > Game center and then signing in with your Apple ID. If you want to make a game center profile you can either:

- Make your profile picture personalized by tapping Edit, and then creating or customizing a memoji.

Or

- Select a nickname by tapping Nickname, enter your name, or select anyone from the suggestions.

For adding your friends, tap friends, tap on add friends, then enter their Apple ID or phone number or a new contact can be added by tapping ⊕.

Game center restrictions can also be set by going to settings > Screen time > Content and privacy restrictions, and then switch on the content and privacy restrictions. After it, choose content restrictions, slide down to the game center, and restrictions can be set.

Fonts can be installed by an app from the app store and then can be managed by going to settings > general, and then tapping fonts.

b. Maintaining health with iPhone 12 Pro Max:

Maintaining health with the iPhone is very easy as the **health app** tracks your total walking time per day and stairs climbing. Moreover, the other data can be manually added to it by tapping on your initials or profile picture in the health app. (If not available, then browse at the bottom of the screen, and slide to the top or tap summary.) You then tap on health details and then edit. After that, tap at the place and enter data, and then tapping is done.

Adding data to a health category is done by tapping browse at the bottom right, the health category screen will appear, then doing either:

- Tapping a category, slide down for all categories.

Or

- Tapping the search field and then putting it in the required category.

(Note: if the health category screen doesn't appear, then tap browse again.)

And then tapping ＞ to update the data, then tapping "Add Data" present at the top-right corner, putting in your information, and then tapping Add or Done.

You can see health and fitness information also; you can see the highlights by tapping the summary at the lower left in the health app and then sliding down to view highlights of your fitness and health data. For the addition or removal of a health category from the favorites, tap summary on the summary screen at the left corner, tap "Edit" for the favorites section, and select a category to switch on or off, and then tap done. To look for the details in the health categories, tap browse present at the bottom right which will show a health category series, tap > you can do the following:

- Change data manually by tapping add data present in the top-right corner of the screen.

- Remove data by tapping show all data below options, swiping left on the record, and then tapping delete. For the removal of whole data tap edit and then delete all.

- Different measurement units by tapping the unit below options and then choosing a changed unit.

- See the allowance of apps to view the data by tapping data sources and access the below options.

- Keep a record of weekly, monthly, and yearly data views by tapping the tabs present at the bottom.

Tracking the menstrual cycle is easy with the health app by tapping browse present at the bottom right, and then tapping cycle tracking and then tapping get started after it; just follow the given instructions. You can check out the tracking options by tapping browse present at the bottom right and then tap cycle tracking after sliding down and tapping options; you'll have options to turn on or off. To see the cycle history and statistics; tap the cycle tracking slide down to view timelines of the recent three periods. Scrolling further will make visible more related statics. To view further details and older info for statistics or cycle history, just tap 〉.

You can see **headphone notifications for the protection of hearing** by going to settings > sounds and haptics > headphone safety, and then turn on notifications. To see their details, you can tap browse in the health app, tap hearing, tap headphone notifications, and then select the notification.

Sleep schedule can be set in the health app by tapping browse, and then tapping sleep, swiping up, and then tapping get started under the "Set up Sleep" and following the given instructions. **Changing a sleep schedule** is done by tapping browse and then sleep. After that, slide down to your schedule, tap edit under next. For the adjustment of schedule for waking up, drag 🔔 and sleeping drag 🛏, selecting any of the alarm options and then tapping done.

Changing the wind-down activities is done by going to sleep in the browse and then tapping the full schedule and options. You'll then have the following options:

- For the addition or removal of an activity tap wind down shortcuts, then tap ⊖ or add another shortcut.
- Selection of sleeping mode to turn on before scheduled bedtime is done by tapping wind down and then choosing a time.

You can set iPhone to **automatically download health data** by tapping your profile picture or name initials at the top right. If not visible there, then try going to the summary and browse and then look there, then tapping health records. You can do the following:

- For setting up the first download tap get started.
- For setting up downloads for other accounts, tap "Add Account".

- Enter the name of the clinic or hospital or look for the nearby organizations; enter the name of the state or city you dwell in.

- To open up a result tap it.

- You can sign-in to your patient portal under "Available to connect".

- Enter the user name and password that is used by you for the portal, then follow the given instructions.

You can **create your medical ID or change it** by tapping at your profile picture, and then tapping Medical ID, and then tapping get started to create a Medical ID or tapping Edit to change the Medical ID. (Note: tapping and holding the health app icon and then choosing a Medical ID will let you view your Medical ID from the home screen quickly.)

Using the **checklist; the health can be maintained**; manage it by tapping your profile picture or initials at the top right, tapping the health checklist, for turning on or learning about an item tap it. To return to the checklist, tap back; after finishing up, tap done.

c. iPhone 12 Pro Max camera:

i.   Learn how to take pics and make videos:

You can **take photos** in photo, time-lapse, video, pano, portrait, and slow-motion modes. To take a photo; go to the camera by tapping 📷 on the home screen or swiping left from the lock screen, it will be opened in a photo mode, and then you can either take a photo by pressing any volume button or by tapping the shutter button.

You **can turn to flash off or on** by tapping ⚡or by tapping ⏶ and then choosing ⚡under the frame to select Auto, Off, or On.

The timer can be set by tapping ⏶, and then ⏱.

You can **take selfies** by tapping the arrows inside the frame; it is done for increasing the field of view. You can also take mirror selfies by going to settings > Camera and then turning on the mirror front camera.

You can **set and lock the exposure** in iPhone 12 Pro Max for upcoming shots by tapping ⏶and then ⊕. You then slide the slider for the adjustment of exposure, and so it locks the exposure until you open the camera again. For the preservation of camera exposure control, to avoid resetting the changes open the camera by going to settings > camera > preserve settings, and then turning on exposure adjustment.

The night mode introduced in iPhone 12 Pro Max is there to enhance the photography experience during night hours by brightening up your shots in low-light situations. In iPhone 12 Pro Max it is also available on the front ultra-wide (0.5x) and wide (1x) camera. You can capture pics with it by choosing photo mode, and then iPhone automatically turns on the night mode. In low-light situations, the ⊙ icon turns yellow and the number appearing beside the ⊙ icon indicates the time required for the shoot. For different experiences with the night mode tap ⊙. After that, put the slider under the frame to select between the Auto and Max timers. The longer time is used by Max, while auto time is selected automatically. The setting is selected for the next night's mode shot as well. You then press the shutter button. (Note: in the mid-capture, if you want to stop taking a night mode shot you can do it by tapping the stop button below the slider.

The crosshairs are visible if the movement is detected by the iPhone, alignment of crosshairs will improve the shot.)

Live photos are taken on the iPhone by selecting photo mode and then tapping ◎, which will turn off or on the live mode. You then tap the shutter button to capture. (Note: the key photos can be changed; bounce and loop effect can be added to it. The sound in the live photo can be muted by opening the live photo, and tapping edit, and then tapping ◎. You'll have the following options:

- Trimming the live video by dragging either end of the frame for the selection of frame the live photo will play.

- Muting a live video by tapping ◀))) present at the top of the screen and then tapping again unmute.

- Making a still photo by tapping the live button for turning off the live feature, a still key photo is formed.

- Setting a key photo by moving the white frame, making the key photo, and then tap done.

For the addition of effects to the live photo, go to the live photo, and after swiping up to view the effects, select one of the following:

- Bounce: by selecting this, the action rewinds forward and backward.
- Long exposure: by selecting this, the blurring motion stimulates a long exposure like a DSLR.
- Loop: this lets the action repeat in a continuous looping pattern.

For **recording a video**, firstly select the video mode, then by tapping on the recording button, or by pressing the volume button it will start recording. You have to press the volume button again to stop recording.

ii. *Learn how to use the features of the iPhone 12 Pro Max camera:*

Taking a panorama photo: this lets you capture shots that you can't see fully on your camera screen. It is done by selecting "Pano mode", and then tapping the shutter button, and then panning slowly in the direction of the arrow. It is kept in the centerline, and then finish up by tapping the shutter button again. Panning in the opposite direction is done by tapping the arrow and to pan vertically, the iPhone 12 Pro Max is rotated to landscape orientation; its direction can be reversed too.

Taking photos with filters is done by choosing photo or portrait mode and then tap ⌃ and then tap ⬤ and then tap under the viewer swiping the filters and then tap one to select.

Taking burst shots will let you select the best one from multiple shots as it captures. You can do it by swiping the shutter button to the left and thus many pics are taken together. A counter displays the number of photos, and then lifting your finger will stop. Choosing photos, you wish to keep is done by tapping the burst thumbnail and then tapping select; the photos to keep are also suggested by the gray dots under the thumbnail. You can then tap the circle in the lower-right edge of each photo and then tap done. The whole thumbnail can be deleted by tapping the thumbnail and then tapping delete.

To take burst shots using the volume up button go to settings > camera, and then switch on use volume up for burst.

There are a few things **you can do while recording a video**:

- Snap a still photo by pressing the white shutter button.

- Zoom in and out by pinching the screen

- A precise zoom by tapping and holding 1x, and then sliding the slider to the left.

(Note: to turn off video recording in HDR mode in your iPhone 12 Pro Max go to Settings > Camera > Record video and then switch off HDR video.)

You can use **quick toggles** for a frame rate and video resolution by tapping quick toggles in the top-right corner; for switching between 4K or HD video recording and for 24, 30, or 60 fps (frames per second) in video mode.

Recording a **quick take video** with which you can take still photos by moving the record button to lock is done by tapping and holding the shutter button in photo mode, and you begin recording a quick take video. Sliding the shutter button to the right and letting go over the lock will make a hands-free recording. The recording can be stopped by tapping the recording button.

You **can record videos in slow mode by tapping** with the front camera. The video can be divided to be played in the slow-mode and normally by tapping the video thumbnail and then tapping edit, after it, sliding the vertical bars under the frame viewer to select the section to be played in slow motion.

Capturing a **sound-lapse video** is done by choosing the time-lapse mode, and then set up your iPhone to the location of a scene in motion. Using a tripod for capturing a time-lapse video will give brightness and more details of a low-light recording.

For **adjusting auto FPS settings,** go to settings >camera > record video, and then tap Auto FPS, and then select Auto FPS to either both 30 or 60 FPS or to 30 FPS only.

To take pictures in portrait mode, and to give studio-quality lighting effects to your Portrait mode pictures; select portrait mode, keenly follow the shown instructions for framing the subject in the yellow portrait box, after that, drag the slider for lightning effect.

- In contour, light highlights and low lights show dramatic shadows on the face.

- The face gets brightly lit with the studio light.

- On a dark background, the face gets spot-lightened using stage light.

- The black and white effect in the stage light is what the photo looks like in the stage light mono.

- The natural light focuses on the face by blurring the background.

- The brightly lit face appears in the natural light with an overall clean look.

And then tapping the shutter button to capture the subject. (Note: the portrait mode can also be removed by going to photos, opening the particular photo, and then tapping edit, and then turning on or off the portrait effect. In iPhone 12 Pro Max while taking photos in portrait mode, the night mode automatically turns on with the wide 1x lens.)

Adjusting depth control in portrait mode by using the depth control slider for the adjustment of the blurring of the background. It is done by selecting portrait mode and then framing the subject, and then tapping ƒ present in the top-right corner of the screen. You can then adjust by dragging it from left to right and then tapping the shutter button.

Adjusting portrait lighting effects by selecting portrait mode and then dragging ⬡to select a lightning effect, then tapping ◉ present at the top of the screen. For the adjustment of the effect drag it from left to right, and then simply tap the shutter button for taking the shot.

iii.   Learn how to set your phone camera:

For the alignment of shots, for displaying photos in a grid; go to settings > camera, and then switch on the grid. After taking a photo the editing tools in the app would be used to align and adjust the shots vertically or horizontally.

The preserve settings include preservation of the last camera mode, lighting, depth, and filter. To avoid resetting the settings when leaving the camera, you can do it by going to settings > camera > preserve setting. You'll have the following options to turn on:

- For the preservation of live photo settings, turn on live photos.

- For the preservation of exposure, turn on exposure adjustment.

- For the preservation of the last setting for lighting option, depth control, or the filter turn on creative control.

- For the preservation of the last Camera mode, turn it on.

You can **take burst shots** by pressing and holding the volume up button.

You can **adjust the volume of shutter sound** using the volume buttons on the iPhone or swiping down from the top-right edge of the screen when the camera is opened. To open the control center and then dragging ◀)), the sound can be muted with the use of the silent/ring switch present on the side. The camera shutter's sound is also muted when the live photo is turned on.

You can **turn off the prioritized faster shooting** by going to settings > camera and then turning off the prioritized faster shooting, which is turned on by default.

The scene detection setting is for the identification of the objects and improving them automatically. It is also turned on by default; you can turn it off by going to the settings > camera, and then turning off the scene detection.

Lens correction is also turned on by default. To turn it off go to settings > camera, and then switch off the lens correction.

The view outside the frame can be turned off as well. It helps in showing the picture in a wide field of view that can be captured. You can turn it off by going to settings > camera > and then turning off the view outside the frame.

The Automatic HDR can be turned off by going to settings > camera, then turning off smart HDR, and then from the camera screen, tapping HDR for turning it on or off.

You can also keep **a non-HDR version** of your photo by going to settings > camera, and then turning on keep the normal photo. (Note: iPhone 12 Pro Max records Dolby vision HDR videos, you can turn it off by going to setting >camera > record video, then turning off HDR video.)

iv.   Learn how to scan a QR code:

Firstly, position the iPhone to be able to do a QR Code scan by opening the camera, the website's link will appear on the screen, tap it to access it. The QR code reader can be opened from the control center by going to settings > control center, and then tapping ⊕ beside the QR code reader. After it, open the control center, tap the QR code reader after positioning the iPhone until the code appears, the flashlight can also be turned on for more light.

d. Using Siri:

For **setting up Siri** go to Settings > Siri and Search, and then you'll have the following options:

- You can either turn on listen and then you can summon it by saying "Hey Siri"
- Or you can press the side button for Siri for summoning it by a button.

You can instead of speaking, **type to Siri** by going to settings > accessibility > Siri, then turning on the type to Siri. For making a request, call Siri, then you can use the text field and your keyboard for asking Siri a question or doing a task.

For **making corrections**, for rephrasing tap ⊙, and then request in a new way. For changing a message before sending, speak

"Change it". For editing your request with text, tap the request, and then type using the keyboard. For spelling out a part of the request, tap ● and then repeat saying your first command, but with the spelling of the word, Siri didn't get in the first place.

To **call Siri**, you can press and hold the side button; when the phone is in silent mode Siri responds silently, but when it is in ring mode, Siri responds with a voice note. While you're connected to EarPods you can hold the center button or call button. After Siri appears, you can either ask it to do a task or simply ask a question. For net question or task, tap ●.

To **use Siri with Airpods**, firstly open the Airpods case, then on your iPhone, go to settings > Bluetooth and then tap ⓘ beside your Airpods list of devices. Choose left or right and then select Siri. However, first check out if the Siri is turned on by going to settings > Siri and Search > and then turning on "Press Side Button for Siri"

You can **respond to messages using Airpods**, announce message lets Siri read the messages when the Airpods are connected. Even if the iPhone is locked, you can simply say "Stop" or "Cancel" or you can remove Airpods from any of them. For replying to the message say "Reply" and then whatever you want to reply. (Note: Siri for confirmations repeats the reply, you can turn it off by going to Settings > Siri and Search > Announce messages, and then turning on reply without confirmation. Also, if the announce message wasn't selected when setting the Airpods it can be done by going to settings > Siri and Search > Announce message and then turning on Announce messages with Siri.)

You can do a few customized settings to Siri:

- You can change the way Siri responds by going to settings > Siri and Search and then you can do the following:

For seeing your requests onscreen, you can do it by tapping Siri responses and then turning on Always show speech.

  - For always seeing the response onscreen from Siri turn on Always show Siri captions in the Siri responses.
  - You can also change the time when Siri responds, by tapping Siri responses and then choosing an option under spoken responses.

- Siri's voice can be changed to male or female by tapping Siri's voice, then choosing any of the voices or accent.
- The apps can be hidden behind Siri by going to settings > Accessibility > Siri and then turning off Show Apps behind Siri.
- There are the following options for the appearance of Siri's suggestions, you can turn them on or off by going to settings > Siri and Search:
    - Lock screen suggestions.
    - Suggestions   when sharing.
    - Home screen suggestions.
    - During search suggestions.
- The Siri's setting can be changed for a specific app by going to settings > Siri and Search, then sliding down and selecting the app.

You can tell Siri some personal things like your relationships, work, and home addresses. For a better-personalized experience; firstly, open the contacts and fill out the contact information. You then go to settings > Siri and Search >My information, tap your name. you can make Siri pronounce your name correctly by saying

"Hey Siri, learn to pronounce my name". Also, you can tell about your relationships.

e. Learn how to use every feature of the calendar:

You can add events by tapping +at the top left, and then after filling in the information tapping add. You can do it by asking Siri as well. Finding events in other apps is done by going to setting >Calendar > Siri and Search and then turning on Show Siri suggestions. Your calendar can be customized by going to settings > calendar and then selecting the desired features. The notifications of the event will let you keep track of events. You can turn it on by going to settings > notifications > calendar then turning on "Allow notifications", then tap the type of event and the place where you want them to appear. For setting a default calendar go to Settings > Calendar > Default calendar.

f. Learn the features of contacts:

Tap + for adding a contact, new contacts are also suggested by Siri. You can turn it off by going to Settings > Contacts > Siri and Search and then turning off "Show Siri" suggestions for contacts. By sharing a contact you'll share all the info on the contact card. For it tap a contact, after tapping share contact, select a sharing method. The contact can be reached quickly for FaceTime, message, call, etc. by tapping a button under the contact's name.

g. Various features of FaceTime:

You can set up FaceTime by going to settings > FaceTime, then turning on FaceTime. The FaceTime live photos should be turned on for the Live Photos during video calls. The email address, Apple ID, and number should be added to use with FaceTime.

You can make a FaceTime call by going to the app and then tapping +, then entering the name or number then either tap video for a video call and audio for an audio FaceTime call. The contact can be selected from your contacts for a call by tapping ⊕. The FaceTime call can be started in the messages by tapping the name or the profile picture and then tapping FaceTime. Up to 32 people can be added to the FaceTime group call by typing the names or numbers one by one in the entry field at the top right in FaceTime. To add a person in the middle of the call, simply tap the screen to open up the controls, swipe up from the top, and then tap to add a person, tap "Add person to FaceTime". A group call can be left by tapping ⊗. You can take a "Live photo" by tapping ⭕during the call with another person, while for a group call, tap the title of the person and then tap ↘ after that, tap ⭕.

h. Newest features of the maps:

The newest cycling directions in the iPhone 12 Pro Max's map is chosen by going to maps and then selecting cycling directions. You can let the map use your precise location by going to settings >privacy > location services and then tapping maps and turning on a precise location. You can select between satellite views, transit, and road by tapping ⓘ then selecting map, satellite, or transit, and then tap ✕.

i. Setting up face recognition and more:

The doorbell and camera can be set, and you can do the following:

- Turning on face recognition in the familiar faces card and then tapping continue.
- Select the person or no one, or everyone to access your photo library.
- And then tap continue after it. Finish the setup for the camera and doorbell.

For knowing the recent visitor with face recognition switched on, go to the home app, tap the Home tab, tap the doorbell or camera then tap ⚙. Tap face recognition, select the recently added person then tap add a name. Enter the person's name and your relationship, select if you want to be notified every time they appear before your camera or doorbell.

j. Translation:

Fonts and languages can be downloaded for offline translations by tapping the translate app, then tapping the language at the top of the screen, and then scrolling down to available offline languages, then tapping the language to download, then tap done.

k. Features of screen timing:

You can see your summary when the screen time is set by going to settings > screen time > see all activity.

You can set screen time by going to settings > screen time, and then turning on the screen time. Tap continue, then tap this is my iPhone, tap downtime then switch on downtime. After selecting customized or every day setting the start and end times.

Chapter 3

Security, Resetting, and Restarting iPhone:

For the protection of your iPhone, don't forget to set Face ID and passcode. You should also turn on "find my iPhone" by going to settings > [name] my device, then after entering your Apple ID tap find my device and then tap turn on "find my device". You can turn on either:

- Finding your device when the battery is critically low using it as your last location automatically by turning on send the last location.
- To locate your device if it is offline by turning on find my network or enable offline finding.

You can also add a family member's device for finding yours.

For **force restarting your device** if it's not working, you can do it by pressing and quickly releasing the volume up button, and then pressing and immediately releasing the volume down button, pressing and holding the side button, just when the apple logo becomes visible releasing the button.

You can **reset your iPhone** by going to settings > general > reset. It'll erase your data and setting; making it just like a brand new iPhone.

Putting it Together

If you have followed this book up to this stage, then your experience is expected to be almost seamless in following this easy introduction to the new iOS 14. The updates that come with the new iPhone 12 contain a lot of useful tools some of which are not immediately obvious except when exposed by a good book like this.

Things like the Triple-lens 3D camera for better video increase the iPhone 12 Pro Max's ability to display high-quality graphics which are appreciated by everyone, including those interested in gaming among other possible demands you may have on your phone.

The detailed and in-depth information in this book has the potential of helping you maximize your use of the iPhone 12 Pro Max's ability to combine the upgraded hardware, iOS, and accessories to use the iPhone 12 Pro Max more productive, a fun device, and a great camera companion. The actionable tips, tricks, hacks, and step-by-step instructions are organized and easy to understand even for a dimwit.

This book was able to cover, but not limited to the following:

• Moving from an Android Device to iPhone 12 Pro Max

• Managing Apple ID and iCloud Settings

• Using the iCloud on iPhone 12 Pro Max

• Taking a Screenshot or Screen Recording

• Sounds and Vibrations

• Home screen and open apps

• Typing and Editing Texts on iPhone 12 Pro Max

• Adding or changing keyboards on iPhone 12 Pro Max

• Using Maps and Translate Application

• Customizing the Control Center on iPhone 12 Pro Max

• Enabling the Features Access from Device Lock Screen

• How to use app clips on iPhone 12 Pro Max

• Activating the iPhone 12 Settings for Travel

• Set up Screen Time for a Family Member on iPhone 12 Pro Max

- Set up FaceTime on iPhone 12 Pro Max

- Collecting Health and Fitness Data on iPhone 12 Max

- Tracking Your Menstrual Cycle on iPhone 12 Pro Max

- Health and Fitness Data on iPhone 12 Pro Max

- Download Health Records in Health On iPhone 12 Pro Max (The U.S. Only)

- Multitasking with "Picture in Picture" on iPhone 12 Pro Max

- New Things Siri can do on iPhone 12 Pro Max

- Using the Compass for the iPhone 12 Pro Max

- A well-organized table of content and index that you can easily reference to get details quickly and more efficiently

Start enjoying your new iPhone 12 Pro Max

Note: This book is not endorsed by Apple, Inc, and should not be considered an official document from Apple.

SPECIAL BONUS

Get this additional Book of Taking Better Selfies with the iPhone 100% FREE!

Hundreds of others are already enjoying insider access to all of my current and future books 100% free!

If you want insider access plus this Taking Better Selfies with the iPhone, all you have to do is **click** https://rebrand.ly/h3edw to claim your offer!